Museum Archives: An Introduction

William A. Deiss

Society of American Archivists
Chicago, 1984

ISBN #0-931828-59-7
Library of Congress Catalog Card #83-050879

Contents

Foreword

"Why should a museum start an archival program?" "How do you go about it?"

To answer these often-asked, important questions, the Society of American Archivists offers William A. Deiss's *Museum Archives: An Introduction,* the third in our series of introductions to archival work in and for particular settings. Previous volumes have dealt with business archives and religious archives.

In all these works, readers will find fundamental rationales for establishing, clear directions for starting, and basic steps for conducting archival programs, capped with solid bibliographies for further reading. For additional guidance and direction, the Society's *Basic Manual Series* offers works on fundamental archival functions, including appraisal and accessioning, arrangement and description, reference and access, security, and surveys, and others on special concerns of archivists, such as automated access, conservation, exhibits, maps and architectural drawings, public programs, and reprography.

In the information age, ready access to data is fundamental. But selecting, preserving, and making available permanently valuable information is essential. The Society is proud to play an important role in accomplishing this goal.

The author of this manual, William A. Deiss, is deputy archivist at the Smithsonian Institution. Others who assisted him in the preparation of the manual include the original committee of reviewers who provided valuable guidance: Edmund Berkeley, Arthur Breton, Elsie Freeman, Catherine Kovacs, Patricia Nauert, and Hugh Taylor. The committee's meeting in Washington was funded by a grant from the National Museum Act. Others who provided help, advice, criticism, and/or encouragement to the author include Ann Abid, James Glenn, Claudia Hommel, Richard H. Lytle, Anita Manning, Mary Elizabeth Ruwell, and Carole Schwartz. The Society is grateful to the author and all who assisted him for the time and talent they devoted to this fine manual.

David B. Gracy II
President

1
Introduction

There are more than 6,000 museums in the United States, but only a small number have archives programs. Most of the museums that have established archives are large and well-funded institutions such as the Detroit Institute of Arts, the St. Louis Art Museum, the Denver Museum of Natural History, the New York Botanical Garden, and the Smithsonian Institution. Most museums in the country, on the other hand, are small and underfunded. The resources of museums vary greatly, but all of them need to make some provision for the preservation of their archival records. A large museum may be able to establish a lavish archival program, while a small museum may have to settle for a modest program; but all museums can set up some kind of program to meet their needs.

The purpose of this manual is to encourage museums to preserve their historically valuable records, and to offer guidelines for the establishment of museum archives. The manual is addressed not to archivists, but to museum professionals with little or no archival training. Although an effort has been made to avoid frequent use of technical terms and archival jargon, some such use is necessary. Therefore a glossary of some archival terms is provided in the following section.

Stack range. *Smithsonian Institution Archives.*

Trustee examining the archives of the Latah County Historical Society, Moscow, Idaho. *Photo by Keith Peterson.*

2
Definitions of Selected Archival Terms

Archives (1) The permanently valuable non-current (inactive) records of the museum preserved because of their continuing value. Archives assume many forms, including machine-readable records and audiovisual materials. (2) The repository where archival records are housed.

Archivist A person responsible for the appraisal, preservation, and reference service of archival materials. In this manual the term is used to describe both the professional archivist and the museum staff member charged with the care of the museum's archives.

Records All correspondence or other recorded information, regardless of media or characteristics, created, received, or maintained by the museum in the course of official business.

Noncurrent Records Records no longer required to conduct current business because they are used infrequently or not at all. Also called inactive records.

Professional Papers Personal research notebooks, correspondence, and other records created by museum staff.

Manuscript Collections Papers collected by archives staff, library staff, or curators from outside the museum for their research value. These are also known as *special collections*.

Provenance The office, administrative entity, or person that created the records. Archives are generally arranged and described on the basis of their provenance.

Appraisal The process by which the archivist determines the value, and thus the disposition, of records based on their administrative, legal, fiscal, or research value.

Records Management That area of general administrative management concerned with achieving economy and efficiency in the creation, use, maintenance, and disposition of records.

Record Series Documents arranged in accordance with a filing system or maintained as a unit in an office because they relate to a particular subject or activity. Records series are created by an office in the normal course of business. They are not created by archivists.

Records Survey The process by which the archivist locates records and determines their current or noncurrent status. The records survey is the first step in records appraisal.

Records Disposition Schedule A document providing guidelines for the retention or disposal of records.

3
Why Should a Museum Have an Archives?

All organizations have a past, a present, and a future. Every museum has an identity that can be defined by its current activities and its purpose; this identity is formed by its past. If a museum is to have an identity it must understand its history, and that history is dependent upon the records created by the museum. Without those records the historian's sources consist only of the memories of individuals and published accounts. If an organization's records have not been preserved one might say it has no history. If no one is responsible for preserving those records, it is almost inevitable that they eventually will be discarded to make space for new records. For a museum's past to be understood, those in charge must ensure that records documenting that past are systematically preserved, and the only way to do so is to establish an archives program.

Nearly all museums, in their role as repositories of artifactual knowledge of culture and cultures, keep some records. Those records are often of permanent value to the institution and should be preserved as archives. An archives program that preserves a record of the past serves many useful purposes for the museum. Archival records serve as an aid in administrative decision making because they contain the collective memory of the museum. They document important transactions and significant administrative decisions that have impact on the current and future activities of the museum. Archives are also important to the museum because they help preserve the documentation of its collections.

Although all (or most) museums attempt to maintain records documenting the acquisition and disposition of objects and specimens in their collections, the records maintained in registrarial files or curatorial files are often incomplete and can be supplemented by tangentially related files in the archives.

Certain types of records must also be preserved to meet legal requirements. Although those requirements may vary from one political jurisdiction to another, there are various types of fiscal records that must be retained, at least for a period of time, in all political jurisdictions. Other records with legal ramifications, such as wills, deeds, and contracts, must also be systematically retained, and an active archival and records management program can aid in that endeavor.

The officers of any organization create records in the course of routine business. Correspondence, minutes of meetings, personnel records, and requisitions are being created daily. Copies are kept and filed because the creators of the documents need to maintain a record of their activities. Minutes of meetings of boards of directors and committees are routinely recorded and kept because decisions must be documented, and because successive meetings will be meaningless unless the group has access to the details of what has taken place at previous meetings. Personnel actions must be documented or there will be no record of an employee's length of service, pay scale, or duties. Financial records must be kept for legal reasons and to maintain budgetary control.

It should be obvious that an organization cannot trust to memory to document its activities and transactions. Everyone keeps files, because the collective memory stored in the files is essential to day-to-day operation. But, as a general rule, as files become older their usefulness in the routine conduct of business decreases. Files that are five years old are generally referred to less than files created the preceding week. Transactions are completed, projects are terminated, buildings are constructed. Such noncurrent records take up valuable space in the office. Why keep six file cabinets when all current files could be kept in one? As files grow older they become less important to the daily routine of the organization, but they do not all become irrelevant or useless. Obviously, not all records should be kept forever. Some files do become useless and should be discarded, because it takes space and costs money to retain them. But files of permanent value should be retained. Efficient administration demands that someone within the organization, with an understanding of the organization's history and its administrative structure, make the decision as to what should be saved and what should be discarded. An archival program can help to

1886 cornerstone box and contents, Cincinnati Art Museum, displayed in the Centennial Exhibition "Art Palace of the West," 1981. *Photo by Ron Forth, courtesy of Cincinnati Art Museum Archives.*

identify and retain the permanently valuable noncurrent records of the organization and to discard the noncurrent records that have no value.

It is not surprising that museum records have research value to historians and other scholars interested in museums, social and cultural affairs, art, science and technology, local and regional studies, and institutional development. Scientists are beginning to use specimen-related records in natural history museums—in conjunction with the specimens themselves—to study floral and faunal distribution, species extinction, and ecosystem relationships. Museums with archives programs are serving an ever increasing number of serious researchers.

Over the past several years museum archives have been used by an increasing number of administrators and curators as well as other scholars. In one instance the director of an anthropological museum in a large eastern city used his museum's archives to learn why a municipal appropriation to the museum had been eliminated several years earlier. Armed with the historical data found in the archives the museum administrators planned to try to regain the funding. Curators at the St. Louis Art Museum found that some records dealing with purchases of works of art a few

Museum archivist Marilyn Ghausi assisting a researcher, 1983. *Courtesy of Museum Archives, The Detroit Institute of Arts.*

decades ago had not been preserved in the curatorial files. A search of the archives yielded the needed information in ledgers produced by the business office. In the mid-1970s curators and architects were asked to prepare for the celebration of the nation's bicentennial by restoring the Smithsonian's Arts and Industries Building (the original United States National Museum) to its nineteenth-century appearance. The task was accomplished using architectural drawings, floor plans, and early photographs of interior exhibit areas found in the Smithsonian Archives. Another museum recently produced a history of its use of volunteers based on extensive research in its archives; and the Bernice P. Bishop Museum in Honolulu has been using its own archives and those of several other museums to compile a history of its collections.

Archival material can also be used to publicize the museum. The public relations value of an archives program cannot be overestimated. A museum with a long history of significant contributions to its nation, state, and community can exploit that history in order to ensure its future prosperity. Budget documents can be

enhanced with historical background statements, statistics, and historical photographs. Fund drives can be strengthened with an appeal to the past, and a history of the museum, perhaps prepared to coincide with an important anniversary in the museum's history, could be an important focus.

Exhibits can be enhanced with historical photographs and documents from the museum's archives. Exhibits documenting the history of the museum can be prepared to recall for visitors the museum's past contributions and, of course, its future potential. In 1981 the Cincinnati Art Museum produced an exhibition on the occasion of the centennial of its founding, together with a brief history of the museum, both of which utilized archival holdings. In the same year the British Museum (Natural History) celebrated 100 years at South Kensington in London with an exhibition and a publication on the history of the museum. The Philadelphia Academy's exhibition of the ornithological art of Louis Agassiz Fuertes was accompanied by a catalog that used archival material at the Academy as well as records of the American Museum of Natural History, the Field

Museum of Natural History, the Herbert F. Johnson Museum of Art at Cornell University, and the New York State Museum.

Art historians have used exhibition and loan records at the Cincinnati Art Museum in an effort to determine the provenance of paintings. Correspondence files of the museum have also proved useful to several historians tracing the careers of artists who had had contact with the museum; and conservators at the museum used early correspondence in an attempt to determine if previous restoration work had been done on certain paintings.

Scientific data in natural history museums is receiving increasing scrutiny from both historians and scientists. Recently, two scholars tracing important specimens collected in the North Pacific Exploring Expedition of the 1850s consulted archival resources at the Smithsonian Institution, the Academy of Natural Sciences of Phila-

delphia, the Peabody Museum of Natural History at Yale University, the Museum of Comparative Zoology, and the British Museum (Natural History).

Conservationists in Canada and Alaska are using field reports of the United States Fish and Wildlife Service and field notes of Smithsonian collectors to prepare reports recommending the establishment of parks, recreation areas, and wildlife preserves. Another scholar is using museum archives throughout the United States to prepare a history of the country's natural history museums.

The value of museum archives is apparent. But despite these successes, the vast majority of museums do not have an adequate archival program. Unless museums begin to do a better job of preserving their archives, much material of value to future generations will be lost.

View of exhibition, "From the Inside: The Archives of The Detroit Institute of Arts, 1883-1945," organized by Marilyn Ghausi, associate archivist, 1980. *Courtesy of Museum Archives, The Detroit Institute of Arts.*

4
Planning a Museum Archives

Any archives has three basic needs: space, staff, and financial support. Any museum director thinking of establishing an archives program must be aware of those needs. The director should determine what the goals are in establishing an archival program, and then decide whether or not adequate space, staff, and support can be provided.

The museum may want its archives to be a major research center for historians of science, technology, or art, or it may simply want to provide adequate care for its historical records. The kind of archives program established should serve the needs of museum staff but should not strain the resources of the museum. A well-funded, well-staffed archival program with sufficient space, supplies, and equipment is obviously preferable. But a modest program, well planned and properly supported, is better than no program at all. An archives program does not have to be lavishly supported in order to be effective, but there will be some costs, and they should be considered in the museum's long-range budget forecasts.

The archives program will have to be staffed, if only on a part-time or volunteer basis. Ideally the archives should be staffed with a professional archivist or someone with training or experience in an archives. At the least, the museum should be prepared to bear the cost of training a current staff member or volunteer to serve as the museum's archivist.

The theory and practice of archives administration may not be as complex or technical as some fields, but it is incorrect to assume that someone automatically becomes an archivist upon being designated the archivist. Training and experience are necessary. Archivists do not simply save old records. Basic principles and techniques have been developed, chiefly in European archives and in the National Archives of the United States, that define the way in which archivists perform their tasks. None of these principles is necessarily inviolable, but each should be understood and experienced in its practical applications by all who hope to call themselves archivists.

Formal training is available through workshops sponsored by the Society of American Archivists (SAA), training classes offered by the National Archives, courses at many colleges and universities, and on-the-job training through internships at many archives.

The professional literature is extensive and growing. This is only one of a series of manuals (many of which are listed in the bibliography) published by the Society of American Archivists. The bibliography also contains other useful publications relevant to museum archives.

The SAA also publishes a quarterly journal, the *American Archivist,* and the Association of Canadian Archivists publishes *Archivaria.*

There are, as well, experienced consultants available who, for a fee, will make recommendations for the establishment or improvement of the museum's program. But, perhaps above all, there are probably archivists in the locality—at state historical societies, universities, or municipal archives—who would be most happy to help with moral support and professional advice. There are also many local and regional archival organizations geared toward helping and training beginners as well as developing professional camaraderie. A list of these organizations is available from the SAA.

The museum must be willing to commit space to an archives program. Archival storage is more efficient than the storage of noncurrent files in file cabinets, boxes, and closets. But some space must be set aside for shelving, staff, and users of the archives.

If costs, space, and staffing are problems, it may be possible from an administrative standpoint to combine some functions. This is not to suggest that the registrar or librarian simply be assigned archival duties, but because of similarities in function, space, and equipment needs, some administrative reorganization might be possible. The registrar, librarian, and archivist are all in the information business, and in some instances the information needs of the museum might be better met by consolidating their functions, based on a review of the museum's needs.

Perhaps several local museums could join in a consortium and pool their funds to establish a central repository for all their records. Costs could be shared, possibly bringing costs for each museum down to a manageable level. Or, perhaps a local repository would be willing to accept, care for, and service the museum's records. Local or state historical societies or nearby university archives should be consulted. Many such depositories collect records of local governments, people, organizations, and institutions. They might be able to provide essential archival services at little or no cost to the museum. This option, however, does not relieve the museum of the basic responsibility of establishing some sort of records program. An outside repository might be happy to receive the archival records but probably cannot operate a records program inside the museum.

5
How to Start an Archives Program

If the museum has the space, the funding, and the commitment to start an archives program, the first step would be to hire an archivist or designate a staff member to serve as archivist. Although a professional archivist will need to become familiar with the museum, little or no training will be necessary. A staff member with no archival training or experience, however, will need courses or workshops in archival theory and practice, and funding must be provided to pay for that training.

Before the archivist can begin, however, the museum must establish some guidelines. First, placement of the archives in the administrative structure of the museum should be clearly identified; the basic authority and responsibility of the archivist must be defined; and, especially in larger museums, an archives committee should be established. Once those matters have been resolved the new archivist should be ready to go to work. The archivist's first step should be to study and master the administrative history of the museum. The knowledge gained should help in planning and conducting a records survey and establishing program priorities. If these actions are accomplished in an orderly manner, the archives program should be well on its way to success.

Placement of the Archives in the Administrative Structure

The archivist should report to the chief administrative officer of the museum, or, in the larger museums, to one of the chief deputies. There should be line authority directly from the central administration. The archives should be an institution-wide concern with authority and responsibility derived from the central administration. Even though the archives might be physically located in the library or in a curatorial unit, the archivist should not be subordinate to the managers of those units. This is true even in a small museum where one person wears nearly all the administrative hats. The archives budget should be a line item in the museum's budget.

Establishing the Basic Authority of the Archives

The archivist's authority should derive from the chief administrative officer or director of the museum. The delegation of authority from the director should be clearly indicated in a memorandum from the director to the staff, trustees, and volunteers, and in an official statement by the director defining the authority and responsibility of the archivist. The statement should point out that all records created by the museum staff in the routine performance of their duties are the property of the museum and that records cannot be discarded or removed from museum property without the express consent of the archivist. The statement should define such terms as "archives," "records," and "personal papers" so that all material of potential archival value is covered. It should include detailed procedures for the transfer and disposal of records, and above all, should make it clear that all staff (whether or not they are on the payroll) have responsibility for the preservation of the museum's archives and that the archives program has the support of the administration. These documents should be issued before initial contact is made with the records-creating offices.

Establishing an Archives Committee

In consultation with the archivist, the director of a large organization will find it useful to establish an archives committee of key staff representing the various curatorial and administrative divisions of the museum. The committee is to give advice and counsel, approve, at least at the beginning, all decisions to discard records, and review records schedules. The committee serves as a source of advice and information for the archivist and as a means of transmitting information between the staff and the archivist. The archivist should work closely with the committee because their help and advice can be extremely valuable.

Many people have an initial suspicion of any new program, especially something like an archives program, that has potential impact on their day-to-day activities. Most of that fear and suspicion can be allayed by properly communicating the goals of the program to the staff, and an archives committee should serve as a vehicle for that communication. An archives committee will also give the staff a feeling of involvement in starting the archives program and will help to provide support for the program.

Studying and Mastering the Administrative History of the Museum

Naturally, if the museum's records are scattered throughout the museum they are difficult to consult, but as a necessary initial step the archivist should learn all that is possible about the history and administrative structure of the museum. The administrative history of the museum is particularly important. Since records are created by people working in official capacities, performing specified tasks within an administrative structure, the records must be interpreted by function. That is, inactive records have little meaning unless it is known who created them, why they were created, what activities or transactions they document, and at what level in the administrative hierarchy they were created. The archivist must understand the history, structure, and function of the agency before the records can be interpreted and appraised. It must be noted that the administrative structure of organizations is rarely static. The most recent organization chart is probably out of date before it is distributed. Hierarchical structures in most organizations are in a constant state of flux. The archivist must thoroughly understand the history of administrative changes in the museum. Good sources are board minutes and by-laws; organization charts; in-house telephone directories, which often list offices in an organizational hierarchy; and annual reports, which often contain staff lists in a hierarchical arrangement. Present and former staff should not be overlooked as sources of information. To reiterate, it is important to learn as much as possible about the history of the museum before trying to deal with its records.

Conducting a Records Survey

Before starting the records survey the archivist should attempt to define a strategy for coverage of the museum. In a small museum that may be solely a matter of starting with the file cabinets in the office and then checking closets, the attic, and the basement. In the larger museum, the initial survey may have to be conducted by mail on a well-designed form, followed up by personal visits. The survey should be followed quickly with appraisal decisions and recommendations for retention or destruction; this provides a product that shows what the archival program can do.

In a large organization it is necessary to keep all of the offices informed of the progress of the survey. Courtesy calls on all offices provide an opportunity to go over the plan of the survey, to describe the pace of work, to discuss priorities, and above all to let the organization's staff know that they are not being ignored but are being scheduled for future attention.

Records surveys should be conducted by the archivist. Each office or records site to be surveyed must be visited personally; the records should be physically examined; and the office staff—the creators and users of the records—should be interviewed. It is the staff that can relate the records to the activity of the office, interpret them, and identify which are current or noncurrent.

Establishing Priorities

A records survey should be followed up with records disposition recommendations as soon as possible. Staff cooperating with the archives on a records survey

should see some results in a short period of time. If a survey of a large museum takes a year to complete, staff members in the first office surveyed will not see results of the survey for a year. In that year they will have created more records, they may have moved records, and they may begin to feel that their cooperation with the archivist was a waste of time. That is not a good start for an archival program that was probably viewed by some with skepticism from the start.

A good archival program takes time to establish. Some offices create records that are more important than others, and those offices must have priority. The archivist must establish reasonable goals and try to meet them. A 100-year backlog of records cannot be dealt with in a few months' time. A good and thorough job done on one record series or one office will serve as a model for future work.

6
Basic Procedures

Records Surveys

The records survey, locating the museum's records and determining if they are in current use or if they are noncurrent, is the first step in records appraisal. Appraisal—the basic and most important function of the archivist—is dependent upon the information gathered in the records survey.

Records surveys are designed to gather information about the documentation pattern of the institution. The same categories of information about the records are gathered from each records-creating unit in the organization. The information gathered is then used as a planning tool by the archivist as well as by the records-creating unit.

The basic categories of information sought in a records survey are (1) the name of the records-creating unit (the office of origin); (2) the names of the records series maintained in the records-creating unit; (3) the date spans of the series; (4) the volume of the series; (5) the arrangement of the series; (6) the current or noncurrent status of the records; (7) the location of the records; (8) the physical condition of the records; (9) the existence of finding aids or indexes; (10) a brief description of the series; and (11) the recommended disposition of the series.

The information sought in a records survey should be entered on a records survey form, which should be filled out as completely as possible by the archivist conducting the survey. A well-prepared form ensures that the surveyor asks the proper questions—both of the records-creating unit and of the records surveyor—and that the information gathered is in a consistent format, enabling compilation of information on an institution-wide basis. There are many survey forms in use, but most are naturally quite similar. The one reproduced in Appendix B is representative. Others can be found in SAA's *Archival Forms Manual*.

Because of their importance, the categories of information sought in the records survey are discussed in detail.

(1) *The name of the records-creating unit* is of particular importance. Records are traditionally identified by their office of origin, because they are often meaningless when viewed outside of the context in which they were created. In the event of changes in office functions or title, the latest office having significant impact on the creation of the records should be named as the office of origin. Predecessor offices should be indicated when necessary.

(2) *The name of the records series* is necessary to identify the file unit being described on the survey form. A record series is defined as "File units or documents arranged in accordance with a filing system or maintained as a unit because they relate to a particular subject or function, result from the same activity, have a particular form, or because of some other relationship arising out of their creation, receipt, or use." A records survey does not attempt to identify individual items, or file folders, but rather identifies records series. Each series is recorded on a separate form.

Examples of records series are: alphabetic correspondence, subject files, budget files, personnel files, and accession records. A records series is usually discernible by the way it is maintained in the office of origin. Offices naturally maintain their records in series. The surveyor does not create the series, but simply perceives it. Unless the office's files are in disarray, records series should be easily recognizable.

(3) *The date span of the creation of the records* should be ascertained by physical examination of the records. Office staff may not know with certainty the date span of their records. A quick examination of the files should produce the date span, i.e., 1941–1957. Uncertainty about the date span should be indicated as *circa* 1941–1957. If the bulk of the records date, for example, from 1948 to 1952, the span can be indicated as 1941[1948–1952]1957.

(4) *The volume of the records* can affect future disposition decisions. Based on this information, the originating office can determine the volume of records that will be discarded, transferred to the archives, or retained; while the archivist can tell how much space the records will take on the shelves if they are transferred.

Knowing the volume of records surveyed also helps if the archivist later returns to the originating office to box the records and move them to the archives. If fewer records are found on the return trip, the archivist knows that some of the records have been moved or discarded.

(5) *The arrangement of the records* is usually easily determined by examining them. Some common types of arrangement are alphabetic by name of correspondent, alphabetic by subject, and chronologic. The arrangement can usually be discerned by looking at file folder headings. Files may also be unarranged.

(6) The archivist must determine *the current or noncurrent status of the records.* As a general rule recently created records are more likely to be in current use than older records, but there are exceptions. The current or noncurrent status of records is usually determined through interviews with the staff in the originating office—the creators and users of the records. The determination of noncurrent status is made jointly between the archivist and the staff of the originating office. If the records receive frequent use they are current and should be retained in the office of origin; if they are seldom or never consulted they should be appraised for transfer to the archives or discarded.

(7) *The physical location of the records* should be noted so they can be found later, after disposition decisions have been made. The location of the records may also have some bearing on their current or noncurrent status. Records stored in file cabinets in the office of the creator are more likely current than those stored in boxes in a closet or warehouse. The location of records should be noted precisely so that, months later, they can be easily found. In some cases a map or diagram might be useful.

(8) *The physical condition of the records* also affects disposition decisions. Records stored under unfavorable conditions might be brittle or mildewed. Those records, if valuable, should be moved to a more suitable location as soon as possible. Records in better condition can be moved at a later date. Records in need of repair or conservation might also be given priority in transfer to the archives. Records infested with vermin must be fumigated before being placed in the archives.

(9) *The existence of finding aids or indexes* should be noted. The office of origin may maintain indexes or folder lists of its files. These can provide the archivist with an aid to later arrangement and description of the records.

(10) *A brief description of the records* should be included. A sentence or two might well be sufficient, and can save much time later on. The description should indicate why the records were created; the function or activity to which they are related; and types of materials found in the records, such as films, photographs, and

audio tapes.

(11) *The recommended disposition of the records* should be noted. It is helpful to indicate whether records are archival or non-archival or whether they should be temporarily retained. This will later serve as a preliminary appraisal.

The records survey provides the basic information which allows the archivist to appraise records for permanent preservation or quick disposal. The knowledge gained from the records survey also aids the archivist in planning. Staff, space, and equipment needs can better be determined if the archivist understands the pattern of records accumulation and the volume of records in the organization.

Appraisal

Based on the information derived from the records survey, and on knowledge of the organizational structure and function of the institution, the archivist decides which noncurrent records will be preserved permanently, temporarily, or not at all. This process is known as appraisal. Although appraisal is often an intuitive, unscientific process, there are certain basic criteria upon which archivists base their appraisal decisions.

The archivist's task is to document the origin, policy, organization, functions, activities, and history of the organization. The archivist must determine if the records being appraised contain that information. If so, they should be retained.

Other records contain information that may have little or no value in documenting the history of the organization, but that is of interest to other parties such as historians, scientists, genealogists, and other researchers. Census records of the United States government are an example. They tell little about how the Bureau of the Census was organized and administered, how it functioned, or how it conducted the census; but they contain enormously valuable data about individuals and groups in American society, and are retained for that reason.

One of the traditional assumptions in records appraisal is that most organizations are based on a hierarchical framework in which the staff perform their day-to-day functions. The records created by the staff of the organization necessarily reflect that hierarchy. This government-based bureaucratic model is based on archival theory developed in European state archives and at the National Archives of the United States. Basically, it is a useful appraisal concept, and is valid for most organizations, including museums. But museums differ in some ways, as do universities and other research-oriented organizations. Many records created at the middle of the museum's organizational pyramid have as much or more value than those created at the apex, because they document specimens or objects, research, and exhibits. It is appropriate here to discuss types of records that should be preserved in any museum. They are:

(1) Records documenting the activities of the governing body (board of directors, regents), particularly minutes of meetings, correspondence, and reports.

(2) Files of the chief administrative officers of the museum: the director, deputy director, and any others who are involved at a relatively high level of policy making in the museum.

(3) Files of curatorial units, departments, curators—files that document the work of the curatorial units, the care of specimens, and research.

(4) Records relating to the physical plant and having permanent value to facilitate the efficient care and maintenance of the buildings that house the museum and its collections.

(5) Records relating to the objects and specimens in the museum's collections. Records relating to the accession of objects and specimens and records relating to transactions involving specimens are usually retained by the museum's registrar. Other records documenting the collections are often retained in the curatorial units, where they can be consulted in close proximity to the collections. They include specimen catalogs; field notebooks; various types of research notes compiled by curators, donors, or researchers as a result of examination of the specimen; and back-up data giving additional information about the object or specimen. Records related directly to specimens rarely find their way to the archives, even though they have permanent value. Accession records rarely become noncurrent because they consist of an ongoing record of transactions affecting the ownership, physical condition, location, loan, sale, and disposition of the object or specimen. Consequently, an accession file created in 1850 could be added to today or tomorrow. The specimen-related records maintained in the curatorial units must be kept with the specimens because they are usually consulted with the specimens. All of these records, even though they are not in the physical custody of the archivist, can be brought under intellectual control as part of the information system maintained in the archives, and can be viewed as part of the total documentation of the museum. The museum archivist must be aware that these records often have research value other than that for which they were created. Just as the records of the director's office might be used by an historian for a reason other than that for which they were created, the specimen-related records often have research value unrelated to specimen documentation.

(6) Records documenting exhibits. The exhibition of objects and specimens is one of the most important functions of museums. Yet many museums make little or no attempt to document the history of their exhibits. Files documenting past exhibits should be brought into the archives from the office of exhibits if one exists, from the curatorial units, or from wherever the files are found. Exhibit catalogs and exhibit scripts are the most common records documenting exhibits. Catalogs often contain photographs of objects on display, and sometimes the text of the catalog may duplicate the script (or labels). But, more often than not, the catalog is not a complete record of the exhibit; the photographic record in the catalog usually includes only some of the objects on display. And it almost never includes a photographic record of what the entire exhibit looked like. How was it mounted? How was it arranged? Where in the building was it located? How much space did it take? How long was it on display? Many of these questions cannot be answered from the kinds of exhibit records traditionally created in the course of planning, mounting, and displaying the exhibit. Museums have been negligent in documenting the history of their exhibits.

The archivist is usually a passive partner in the creation of records. Most archivists simply appraise records that have been created by others. They decide which records are noncurrent, which have permanent value, which are retained, and which are destroyed, but they rarely become involved in the creation of records. But exhibition records is one area where the archivist should take a more active role. Museum archivists should urge that the museum make a systematic photographic record of all exhibits, in addition to the records traditionally generated. The museum archives should be the depository for a complete history of all exhibits. After all, a museum without exhibits is simply not a museum, and a museum that cannot document the history of its exhibits, the history of its intellectual and aesthetic output to its public, and the history of the use of its internal building space, cannot document one of the most important facets of its history and the cultural history of the community it serves.

(7) Information files assembled by curators relating to the objects in the collections or to the kinds of objects in the collection. Curators in a railroad museum, for instance, might maintain files that not only document locomotives or boxcars in their collection, but also contain various kinds of information on the history of railroads, rail technology, and blueprints and specifications for diesel engines. This type of file might contain brochures, technical manuals, obituaries, blueprints, railway schedules, and ticket stubs, and might also contain collected manuscript items, or correspondence of the curatorial staff with historians of technology, well-known figures in the history of railroading, or railway buffs. This correspondence, filed into the information file because of its content, might never find its way into what the archivist would assume is the correspondence file of the curatorial unit. That correspondence file, therefore, is not a complete record; fragments of it are in another location, in a different record series. The archivist must develop descriptive techniques to gain intellectual control over the records and to make them accessible to potential users.

There are basic principles to follow in appraisal, but none can substitute for a knowledge of the administrative history and structure of the organization, the patterns of records generation and information flow, and common sense. Not all records can be saved. If worthless or seldom used records are retained, the future researcher is faced with an insurmountable pile of source material to wade through in search of valuable information. Furthermore, the costs of saving unimportant records must be considered. Space and staff cost money, and a determined effort must be made to save only those records that have permanent value, if for no other reason than to ensure the maximum use of always limited budgets.

Accessioning

Just as specimens and objects brought into the museum's collections must be accessioned, so must records placed in the archives. Objects and specimens are accessioned by the registrar or, perhaps, the curatorial staff; but the records placed in the archives should be accessioned by the archivist, who should maintain a separate record of accessions. Records placed in the archives should not be viewed in the same way as objects or specimens acquired for the museum's collections. The museum is not *collecting* its archives; rather, it is *maintaining* them. The records in the archives should not be considered part of the museum's collections, and should not be treated as such. Records should be accessioned at the record series level, and rarely as individual items.

The archivist bringing records into the archives should create a record of the transaction. It may be weeks, months, or years before the records are fully processed, but a record of their acquisition and location in the archives must be maintained.

Much of the information maintained in the archives accession register is the same as or similar to the information found on the records survey form. An archives accession form is recommended, with blanks to be filled in or boxes to be checked off as the records are accessioned. Basic information needed includes:

(1) *An accession number.* Any type of numbering system is acceptable as long as it works—that is, if it leads to the information necessary to document the accession transaction. A numbering system might start with 1 and be continued infinitely, or it might be consecutive by year. For instance, the first accession in fiscal year 1982 receives the accession number 82-1, the next accession is 82-2, etc. It is a simple system that facilitates filing of accession sheets and ensures that accession dates can easily be ascertained and that accession numbers will not become too unwieldy.

(2) *Date of accession,* together with the name of the archives staff member who received it.

(3) *Office of origin.* In a formal sense, institutional records transferred to the archives from an office within the organization have no donor; the office has simply transferred records to the archives. The individual who was the contact in the office, or who authorized the transfer, should be noted, but that individual is not the donor of the records. A donor is one who owns records, and by definition employees, no matter what their level, do not own the organization's records; they are the creators and the custodians of the records. If the archives is collecting primary source material from outside the museum to aid in curatorial research on the objects and specimens, the donor would be noted here. Such manuscript collections, of course, should be accessioned and maintained entirely apart from the museum's archives.

(4) *Type of transfer.* It should be indicated whether the accession is a transfer of official records or a donation from an individual or organization.

(5) *Documentation.* Any documentation in addition to the accession register should be included. Are the records scheduled for destruction or permanent retention? Is there a deed of gift, if one is necessary? Has receipt of the records been acknowledged?

(6) *Restrictions.* Any restrictions on the use of the records should be noted.

(7) *Records series title.*

(8) *Inclusive dates.*

(9) *Arrangement.* Is the file alphabetic, and if so by name, or subject? Is it numeric?

(10) *Volume.* How big is the accession? A standard unit of measure, such as cubic feet, helps in comparing quantities.

(11) *Finding aids.* Are there any finding aids already in existence? Perhaps the office of origin had a file plan, or a folder list. Any available aids should be noted.

(12) *Forms of materials.* Are there any oversize materials, photographs, machine-readable records, maps, charts, blueprints, or objects?

(13) *Preservation needs.* If the records have deteriorated because of poor storage or care, their condition might determine processing or conservation priorities. Perhaps vermin are present and fumigation is necessary. If so that should be noted and taken care of before the records are placed in the archives, lest other records be infested.

(14) *Shelf location.* Even though the records may not be processed and assigned a final shelf location for some time, they must have a temporary location, and that location should be noted. Any system used for temporary shelving should be consistent, and should be closely monitored.

(15) *A brief description of the records should be prepared,* indicating their provenance and the reason for which they were created. One or two sentences or a paragraph should be sufficient; for example: "These records were created by the director of the museum as secretary of the board of regents. They include minutes of board meetings, agendas, reports to the board by the director, and correspondence of the director with the board of regents."

A sample of an accession form is reproduced in Appendix C.

Arrangement and Description

If appraisal is the basic function of the archivist, arrangement and description follow closely behind. The archivist who appraises the records determines what will be saved, while the archivist who arranges and describes them determines, in a sense, whether or not they will be used.

Arrangement and description are the essence of archival work. More time is spent in an archives on arrangement and description than on any other task— probably more than on all others combined. Arrangement and description is the process (or processes) by which records are made accessible to potential users. Records, after all, are saved because they have permanent value. If they are not accessible, are in disarray, or are not made known to potential users, they might as well be discarded. Appraisal decisions are irrelevant if records are not properly arranged, described, and made available to users after they have reached the archives.

Arrangement and description basically constitute one step in the processing of archives. (The term "processing," however, is sometimes used as a synonym for arrangement and description.) Generally, records are considered to be processed when they have been arranged, described, boxed, put in folders, and placed on the shelf and are ready for use by researchers.

Most archivists follow two basic principles of archival

Processing records in the archives of The University Museum, University of Pennsylvania, Philadelphia.

arrangement: the principle of provenance, or *respect des fonds,* and the principle of sanctity of the original order. The principle of provenance states that archives of a given records creator must not be intermingled with those of other records creators. The principle of sanctity of the original order requires that if records arrive in the archives in a discernible order—the order imposed on them by the creating agency—that order must be maintained.

These two principles are basic to archival theory as it has developed in Europe and America over the last century. Not only are there legitimate theoretical bases for these principles, but they simplify the tasks of arrangement and description.

The principle of provenance recognizes the fact that records are created by organizations or individuals in the course of conducting business. Therefore, the records document the activities of that organization or individual. Whatever their informational content might be, they have meaning only in the context in which they were created.

The principle of the sanctity of the original order recognizes that records maintained in an organizational unit or by an individual generally are arranged in such a way that they are useful to the creator. The arrangement of the files reflects the functions and organizational structure of the office or individual that created them. Rearrangement probably would obscure the functioning of the office.

Top right: View of Concincinnati Art Museum archives stacks before processing, 1979. *Bottom right:* View of Cincinnati Art Museum archives stacks after processing funded by a grant from the National Historical Publications and Records Commission, 1980. *Photos courtesy of Cincinnati Art Museum Archives.*

There is also a pragmatic reason for observing the principles of provenance and sanctity of the original order: they facilitate arrangement and description. An explanation of the provenance of the records helps describe them. That is, they can be described as the records of the Office of _____. The title of the record unit in effect helps describe the record unit. If there is a discernible original order to the records, why disturb it? The records are already arranged—why rearrange them if it is not necessary? Recognition and description of the original order is easier, less time-consuming, and more utilitarian than rearrangement. Archivists do not deal with preconceived arrangement schemes. Records do not have to be alphabetic, or chronologic, or subject-oriented. There is no *right* way to arrange records. Records are arranged by their creators. Archivists should discover and describe that arrangement, not rearrange the records. Arrangement (or rearrangement) should be performed by the archivist only when necessary. Files that are rearranged under some arbitrary standard, or that are disarranged or split up, are said to have lost their integrity. This means they have lost their organic unity; they no longer document the activities and functions of their creating office, and the researcher can no longer be sure that they are a complete record.

UNIVERSITY MUSEUM - ARCHIVES

Folder Title Listing

Record Group: Mediterranean   Subgroup: Underwater Archaeology

Series: Yassi Ada   Initials/Date: CAN & KTB Sep. 10, 1981

Box Number	Folder Title
1	Stereo Photographs of Byzantine Shipwreck 7th A.D. Traverse A
	Stereo Photographs of Byzantine Shipwreck 7th A.D. Traverse B
	Stereo Photographs of Byzantine Shipwreck 7th A.D. Traverse C
	Stereo Photographs of Byzantine Shipwreck 7th A.D. Traverse D
	Stereo Photographs of Byzantine Shipwreck 7th A.D. Traverse E
	Stereo Photographs of Byzantine Shipwreck 7th A.D. Traverse F [contact prints, enlargements]
	contacts [enlargements]
	Byzantine wreck (7th A.D.) [grid photos and drawings]
	Misc. contacts
	Contacts - Arranged by object
	Contacts - Arranged by object [Photos]
	Neolithic Figurines - Eutresis [Photos]
2	Grid #4: Frame #1, Sector B and C
	Grid #5: Frame #1, Sector B
	Grid #6: Frame #1, Sector B
	Grid #7: Frame #1, Sector B
	Grid #37: Frame #4, Sector B
	Grid #38: Frame #4, Sector C July 21
	Grid #39: Frame #3, Sector B
	Grid #40: Frame #3, Sector C
	Grid #41: Frame #3, Sector B
	Grid #42: Frame #2, Sector B July 29
	Grid #43: Frame #4, Sector B July 29
	Grid #44: Frame #5, Sector B July 30
	Grid #45: Frame #5, Sector C July 31
	Grid #46: Frame #4, Sector A July 22
	Grid #46: Frame #5, Sector A July 31
	Grid #47: Frame #1, Sector B
	Grid #48: Frame #1, Sector C Aug 1
	Grid #49: Frame #1, Sector C Aug 2
	Grid #50: Frame #1, Sector B Aug 2
	Grid #51: Frame #1, Sector B Aug 7

Finding aid developed for a museum archives. *The University Museum, University of Pennsylvania, Philadelphia.*

Records can be described at the record unit level (see definition below), the series level, the file folder (or file unit) level, or the item level. Most finding aids or inventories describe records at the series, container, or file folder level, but even brief descriptions at the record unit level are helpful. Each archivist must decide the level at which the records will be described. Arrangement and description are time-consuming and costly. It is better to have a minimal level of control over all the collections rather than in-depth control of one or two collections and no control of many others.

Description at the record unit level. The archivist determines the units in which arrangement and description take place. The term "record unit," as used here, is defined as a body of records produced by a particular office (or individual) over a specific period of time, in the course of conducting its business or pursuing its function.* A safe assumption is that a record unit will be created by an office that appears in the organization chart. Within that office different series of records will be maintained. For instance, the records of the director of the museum form a record unit, which might be divided into an alphabetic correspondence series, a subject file series, appointment books, budget files, and administrative files. All of those files are separate series of the record unit.

Most techniques of archival description are designed to describe bodies of records, not individual items. Archives are not described and controlled as books in a library or as individual museum specimens. Archives are described as aggregates of material. An example of description at the record unit level, taken from the *Guide to the Smithsonian Archives, 1978,* is shown on page 22.

Using the example as a model, the elements of description of the record unit level are as follows: The title of the record unit and the dates of the records are on the first line. The number in parentheses at the upper right is the record unit number, which indicates the shelf location of the records. The second line indicates that the record unit consists of *records* of the Division of Reptiles and Amphibians, and it also includes an indication of the volume of the records. The first three paragraphs of the description consist of the administrative history of the originating office, in this case the Division of Reptiles and Amphibians of the National Museum of Natural History. If these were the papers of an individual, the administrative history would be replaced by a biographical sketch. The administrative history describes the functions of the originating office and

gives names of the officers responsible for the creation of the records.

The next paragraph describes the records. It is called the descriptive entry or the scope and content note. The arrangement section indicates the series into which the record unit is divided. Those series were created by the originating office, not artificially established by an archivist. Series would have been created by the archivist only if the records were in disarray and needed to be arranged before they could be used. The finding aids section indicates that a more detailed description of the record unit is available. That description consists of a box and folder list or inventory.

Even though a more detailed description of these records exists, the guide entry reproduced here gives the potential user enough information to know if the records should be consulted, and also indicates the arrangement of the records in such a way as to identify which portion of the collection might best be examined. It must also be noted that much of the information included could have been taken directly from the records survey form and the accession register. If the staff is pressed for time it is much better to gain this level of control over many record units than to seek detailed item-level or folder-level control over a few collections.

Arrangement at the box, folder, and item level. Most archives are maintained in acid-free document cases, which come in both standard and legal sizes. The standard size box is 7 inches high, 12 inches long, and 5 inches wide; the legal size is 7 inches high, 15 inches long, and 5 inches wide. File folders, which also should be acid-free, are placed upright in the box, just as they would be in a file drawer. Each file folder should be

Archives of the Latah County Historical Society, arranged in file folders. *Photo by Keith Peterson.*

_____

*I use the term "record unit" as a convenience for any body of records below the repository level and above the series level. It includes records groups, subgroups, etc.

(*161*)

Division of Reptiles and Amphibians, 1873-1968
Records (11.3 cubic feet).

The collection of reptiles and amphibians under the care of the Smithsonian Institution had its origins in the collection of Spencer F. Baird, which he presented to the Institution when he came to Washington to accept the position of Assistant Secretary in 1850. For the next three decades there was no curator officially in charge of the collection, and most of the early publications resulting from the collection were produced by Baird and Charles Frederic Girard, who from 1850 to 1860 was Baird's chief assistant.

In 1879 Henry Crecy Yarrow, an army surgeon who had served as naturalist on the United States Surveys West of the 100th Meridian led by Lieutenant George Wheeler, was appointed Honorary Curator of the Department of Herpetology, a position which he filled on a part-time basis until his resignation in 1889. During the early 1880's the Department was known variously as the Department of Herpetology, the Department of Reptiles, and the Department of Reptiles and Batrachians. By about 1885 the latter title had become standard. In 1947 the name was changed to the Division of Reptiles and Amphibians.

Curators since 1889 have included Leonhard Stejneger, Curator, 1889-1943, and Doris Mable Cochran, Assistant, Associate, and full Curator, 1927-1968. James A. Peters, Associate Curator, 1964-1966, became Curator in 1966.

The records contain general correspondence of the Division's curators; Leonhard Stejneger material pertaining to the international congresses he attended as a representative of the United States National Museum; and administrative memoranda regarding the National Museum operations for the Division of Reptiles and Amphibians and the Departments of Biology, Vertebrate Zoology, and Zoology, pertaining to requisitions, budgetary matters, publication policy, expeditions of curators, museum exhibitions, and personnel matters. For additional records of the Division of Reptiles and Amphibians, see the Leonhard Stejneger Papers, record unit 7074 and the James A. Peters Papers, record unit 7175.

ARRANGEMENT: (1) General correspondence, incoming and outgoing, 1873-1968; (2) outgoing correspondence, 1882-1883, 1889-1922; (3) correspondence related to scientific congresses, 1895-1911; (4) administrative memoranda, 1946-1966. FINDING AIDS: Description in control file.

separately marked and identified with the record unit number, the box number, and a folder number, in addition to information on the tab identifying the contents of the folder. For instance, a folder might be marked on the front as part of Record Unit 50, box 14, folder 9, and the information on the tab might indicate "Correspondence, A–B, 1935." In this way the folder is sufficiently identified that it can be easily returned to its proper location if it is inadvertently misfiled or misplaced.

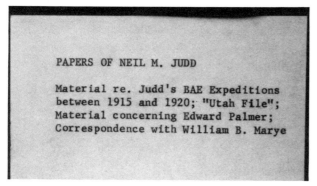

```
PAPERS OF NEIL M. JUDD

Material re. Judd's BAE Expeditions
between 1915 and 1920; "Utah File";
Material concerning Edward Palmer;
Correspondence with William B. Marye
```

Box label. *National Anthropological Archives, Smithsonian Institution.*

If time permits, items in the folder should be arranged if the original order is not discernible, or if the file has been disarranged. In many cases an alphabetic arrangement is called for; in some cases it should be chronologic; and often it is a combination of the two. For instance, the sample folder listed above contains "Correspondence, A–B, 1935." Normally one would expect that when the folder is opened the correspondence starts with A on top and continues through B at the bottom. Within the A's, Mr. Anderson is placed before Mr. Arthur. If there are several pieces of correspondence with Mr. Anderson, both incoming and outgoing, then normally the most recent piece is on top, with the earliest piece on the bottom. There are no "rules" calling for such arrangement, but this is conventional practice.

Foreign objects should be removed from the items. Paper clips, staples, and rubber bands are usually damaging to the paper as they deteriorate. Straight pins must always be removed because of the danger they pose. They should be replaced, if necessary, with stainless steel paper clips, which do not deteriorate.

Making the records available. Reference and access to the records will be discussed in the next section of this manual, but there is an essential final step in the arrangement and description—or processing—of records. Potential users need to know that the records exist. A museum archives has two main constituencies: museum staff and outside researchers. As the official memory of the museum, the archives will frequently be consulted by museum staff. But unless they know what the archives contains, staff and researchers cannot make use of the resources. The staff and administration of the museum must be made aware of the archives and its holdings. Finding aids to the records of a specific office should be sent to that office, new accessions should be announced in the museum's newsletter, an annual report of archives activities is recommended, and personal contact must be maintained with staff in all records-creating units.

Potential outside researchers must also be made aware of the existence of the holdings. Acquisitions should be announced in appropriate scholarly journals, entries describing non-administrative records of the museum should be submitted to the National Union Catalog of Manuscript Collections (NUCMC) published by the Library of Congress, and entries should be submitted to any other appropriate guides to archives and manuscript collections in each field.

Reference and Access

Records surveys, appraisal, and arrangement and description are all part of the process of locating and preserving the historically valuable records of the museum. But, there is no point in preserving archival materials unless they will be made available to potential users.

Much reference service will be in response to written or telephone inquiries. But some researchers will need to visit the archives to consult the records. The fastest and surest way for a new archives program to build a constituency is through reliable and helpful reference service. The archivist's primary reference responsibility is to the administrators, curators, and support staff of the museum, and the best way to cultivate support for the archives program is to provide the best possible reference service. Visiting researchers are also extremely important, but generally they can be expected to do more of their own research.

A researcher visiting the archives will find it useful to fully describe the nature and scope of his inquiry. The archivist, with an acquired knowledge of the records and the pattern of documentation in the museum, can often lead the researcher to specific records. While finding aids and indexes to the records are necessary, they cannot substitute completely for the archivist's personal knowledge of the records. Much of the successful research done in archives is a result of the cooperation of the archivist and the user. Perhaps the most personally rewarding result of all the archivist's work is in helping researchers find information in the archives. The archivist must help the researcher as much as possible, but the records must be protected against damage, mutilation, disarrangement, and theft. Steps must be taken to protect the records without creating an uncomfortable atmosphere for the researcher or discouraging use of the archives. Recommended procedures for controlling access to the records include:

(1) The records storage area should be closed; a member of the staff should retrieve the boxes and make them available to the researcher.

(2) The archives should keep a record of researchers, including museum staff and administrators, and of the materials made available to them. A registration form (see examples in the SAA *Archival Forms Manual*) will help track uses and users for security of the records and statistical information on use.

(3) The researcher should use the material at a table, cleared of all other papers, that can be supervised by a staff member at all times. If the museum has a library, the archives may share the reading room. A large museum may be able to establish a separate reading room or search room that can be monitored through a glass wall from the work or reception area.

Research table and map cases. *The University Museum, University of Pennsylvania.*

In addition, the use of some records must be restricted in order to ensure the privacy of the museum and its personnel. Private museums have no obligations—other than to scholarship—to allow use of any of their records, while museums funded or administered by federal, state, and local governments might be legally obliged to fulfill particular requirements.

Any institution has a right to maintain its privacy, but museums exist in order to disseminate information, and therefore should make every effort to open their non-current records to scholarly use. Restrictions are usually negotiated with the office of origin, but it is advisable to establish a museum-wide policy through discussion with

the museum's administration and legal counsel. Exceptions to the policy should be made only in extraordinary circumstances. A reasonable policy might be that all records more than fifteen years old are open to researchers (with some exceptions, such as personnel records) and that any records in the archives that are less than fifteen years old may be used only with the permission of the originating office. Whatever the restrictions policy is, it should be uniform and it should be administered consistently. Records that are made available to any outside scholars should be available to all. It is unethical to close records to some scholars while opening them to others. The archivist should be aware of copyright laws and should administer restrictions accordingly.

All persons wishing to quote from museum records in publications should be required to write for permission. This allows the archivist to check for any restrictions or copyright problems, and also informs the archivist of publication from the records. Such data are useful in the annual and other reports of the archives.

Scholarly use of the archives should be publicized, particularly within the museum. An annual report, for instance, could contain a section on use of the archives, including reports on research in progress and lists of publications resulting from research conducted in the archives.

Records Management

The effort to preserve the museum's archives can be enhanced by the development of a records management program which is concerned with the "life cycle" of records from their creation until their final disposition. The basic concern of the archivist is the preservation of the permanently valuable noncurrent records of the organization. An effective records management program can help achieve that goal in an orderly fashion.

Records management in large organizations or governmental entities can become incredibly sophisticated, involving forms management, development of information systems, control of word processing equipment, standardization of computer hardware, and efficiency of mailroom operations. In most museums, however, the archivist can hope only to employ some basic records management techniques to help ensure the orderly disposition of records.

As discussed earlier, appraisal decisions are based on a knowledge of the organization's structure and function, its administrative history, and the information gained in the records survey. Appraisal is the process of deciding which records will be permanently preserved (that is, which are archival), which will be discarded because they have no permanent value (non-archival), and which records will be preserved for a specified period of time and then discarded. The latter records have no archival value but must be retained for a period of time after they become noncurrent—usually because of legal needs or requirements. These records may be stored by the archives, but they never become part of the archives. In effect the archivist operates a records center where noncurrent records of temporary value are stored for a specified period of time, at the end of which they will be discarded in an orderly manner based on records schedules established by the archivist in the capacity of records manager.

The records schedule defines the process of records disposition. Some records series recur throughout the institution, and others will be unique to a specific office, but within that office they will probably continue to be produced, used, and maintained, and will become noncurrent in a continuing process. It is the archivist's job to understand the process and help manage it in a way that will ensure the orderly creation, maintenance, and disposition of records.

In a large organization, many kinds of finanical and housekeeping records are maintained in each office and in a central file or in summary form at a higher level in the hierarchy. In the course of records appraisal the archivist will accumulate enough information to discern the pattern of records creation and maintenance in the organization. It will become apparent that certain kinds of records are duplicated in various files. Personnel files, for instance, are maintained in the museum's personnel office, with duplicates of pertinent files maintained for convenience by each departmental office. Requisitions and purchase orders are retained by the office of supply services, with duplicates retained by individual offices. Budget files are routinely maintained in every office. When these records become noncurrent they may need to be retained permanently or temporarily (depending on the appraisal decision), but they need not be retained in multiple copies. The archivist, based on knowledge of the documentation patterns of the museum, should designate for each series an office of record, the files of which will be retained because they constitute the most complete or summary record of transactions. Duplicate files in other offices or routine housekeeping records summarized in the office of record can be discarded based on record schedules provided by the archives.

Just as archivists try to eliminate the preservation of duplicate records, they also try to eliminate the preservation of records that document routine transactions in great detail. Often such records are maintained in a digested or summary form at another (usually higher) level in the institution. Financial records of various sorts are probably the prime example. The large museum has a budget formalized in a document showing funds allocated to each administrative unit. Each unit might also have a copy of that budget, as well as a copy of its individual budget submission and back-up data accumulated in the course of formulating the submission. Over the course of the year the office will also keep requisitions, purchase orders, and accounts documenting its expenditures—records that document purchases of everything from paper clips to typewriters, supplies, and travel. It is likely that all of these expenditures are also documented in the accounting office or the central supply office, and that none (or very few) of them has any permanent value. Twenty years later administrators or historians may be interested in how much money was allocated to a curatorial division or an administrative office, but not in how much that office spent on paper clips or typewriters. The information has more value, takes less space to store, and is easier to use in summary form. Records schedules are the tool to indicate which of these records should be preserved and which should be discarded. In most organizations only a small portion of records created have permanent value. Records management techniques can aid the archivist not only in saving those records with permanent value, but in ensuring the orderly disposition of those records with no permanent value.

Space Needs and Equipment

The storage and use of the permanent records of the institution should be given as much care and attention as the artifacts and specimens in the museum's collections. Acid-free boxes and folders, steel shelves, moderate and stable temperatures, fire prevention devices, and security precautions will go a long way to help preserve archival materials. In a small museum work and reading areas may have to be shared with other similar museum functions. In a larger museum the specific storage requirements and space needs of the archives can be met through facilities designed for the preservation and use of records.

Conservation and Supplies

Museum professionals are well aware of conservation needs. Specimens and objects are often received in a deteriorated condition in need of restoration and repair. Even objects and specimens in perfect condition must be preserved and stored in such a way that they will not deteriorate. Since most museums engage in conservation as a routine part of their program, I will not discuss needs and techniques in detail.

There are, however, some ways in which archival material must be treated differently than museum objects. Specimens, objects, and artifacts are usually

Archives stored in acid-free boxes are retrieved with the help of a book cart. *National Anthropological Archives, Smithsonian Institution.*

viewed as discrete items. One museum may have a shrunken head that needs restoration, another a valuable painting, or a bird skin, or an airplane or tractor in need of repair. Each is treated as an individual object and dealt with as necessary.

But archival materials are usually found as aggregates. On the average, one cubic foot of files (approximately half of a file drawer) contains 2,000 sheets of paper. A modest archives, therefore, includes many more items than a large museum. Most of the pieces of paper within a folder of records have value only in relation to the other pieces of paper, which as a unit make up the body of records. The pieces of paper do not usually have intrinsic value, but they possess a collective value, because of their informational content—a value that inheres in the records as a unit, not as discrete items.

The archivist, in conserving aggregates of records, needs to (1) find the records; (2) appraise them, and if they have permanent value, bring them into the archives before they rot or are discarded or lost; (3) fumigate them if there is any evidence of vermin; (4) remove foreign objects such as paper clips, staples, and rubber bands, which, as they deteriorate, damage the records;

(5) remove them from their old file folders and place them in acid-free folders; (6) box them in acid-free document containers; and (7) if appropriate, microfilm the records to preserve their informational content or to provide use copies of fragile records that might be damaged by handling.

The necessity for placing archival materials in acid-free (or acid-neutral) folders and boxes has been mentioned previously for, along with temperature and humidity controls, it is one of the foundations for the effective, long-term conservation of archival materials. Most file folders used by offices (and most cardboard boxes) have a high acid content as a result of economies in the papermaking process. This acid will migrate to adjacent pieces of paper and, over a period of time that may be as short as twenty years, will significantly deteriorate both the folder and its archival contents. Over time, the folders and documents will crumble into dust.

Microfilm is widely used as a means of preserving the informational content of records in lieu of the paper documents. The staff costs of preparing materials for microfilming and the technical requirements for archival quality film are such that this tool must be approached cautiously.

Polyester encapsulation may be used to provide physical support to fragile and brittle documents. This encapsulation table is in The University Museum, University of Pennsylvania, Philadelphia.

Oral History

Oral history can be a valuable adjunct to an archives program. Well-planned interviews conducted with current and former staff members, trustees, or donors can supplement the records maintained in the archives. Oral history interviews can (1) document the beginning of the museum or of various programs and activities that generated few records; (2) fill gaps in records; (3) increase knowledge of decision making and the discussions that led to decisions, because the final record often reflects consensus, not the process of arriving at the consensus; (4) aid in the solicitation of records and manuscript collections; (5) provide contact with potential donors; (6) aid in public relations; (7) establish close personal ties with the archives' constituents; (8) develop a sense of history within the museum; and (9) present a balanced viewpoint of events not fully documented in the records.

Oral history is popular and flashy, and the information gained from a well-planned and well-administered program can be extremely useful. But there are trade-offs. When conducted properly, oral history is expensive and time-consuming. An oral historian must be hired, or a member of the museum staff must be trained in oral history techniques and procedures. Equipment and space must be provided; and the production of useable tapes or transcripts will be slow. It may require up to sixty hours of research, processing, and transcription for every hour of tape produced. It is up to the museum to decide if oral history ranks high enough on the list of priorities. For more information, several recommended readings are listed in the bibliography.

Manuscript Collections

Many museum archives also contain collections of materials that are not records of the museum. These may consist of personal or professional papers of museum curators or files of organizations or other people. Such materials are often collected by the museum archivist or curators, or may come to the museum because they are associated with objects or specimens in the collections. These collections are not, strictly speaking, archives of the museum, but are known as manuscript collections or special collections.

The principal difference, for the archivist, is in accessioning procedures. Any materials brought into the archives that were not originally the property of the museum should be accompanied by a deed of gift from the donor. The deed of gift should indicate that the material is the property of the museum and that copyright is transferred to the museum. Any restrictions on use of the material should be spelled out, and the document should be signed by both the donor and the archivist (or a designated official of the museum). In general, manuscripts should not be accepted on loan or if they are not going to be available to researchers.

The techniques for description and care of manuscript collections are basically the same as those for archival records. Many collections arrive at the archives with a definite provenance and in an original order, and there is usually no reason to rearrange them. Care of the materials is the same as that of archival records. They should not be intermingled with other collections or with archival records, but should be maintained as units.

Manuscript collections are administered by many archival programs and are a valuable research resource. Any museum starting an archives program may want to consider collecting outside of its own walls. But priorities should be determined before embarking on such a project. The museum should establish a program for the care and preservation of its own records before collecting other manuscript materials.

Outreach and Public Programs

Museum archivists should seek to develop a constituency and should ensure that the holdings of their archives are made known to that constituency. The archivist must publicize the program, and that can be done in several ways. Within the museum the archivist can produce exhibits using materials from the archives and can work with curators to determine whether archival material can be used in exhibits they are planning. Announcements of new accessions and other news from the archives can be published in the museum's newsletter. Annual reports can be produced and distributed throughout the museum. The report should include summaries of activities, accessions, future plans (if appropriate), and research in progress, as well as a bibliography of publications that have resulted from research done in the archives. The archivist should bear in mind, however, that good reference service is also a form of outreach. If the archives provides good service, word will get around the museum; and there is no better form of publicity for an archives program.

The archivist should also make the holdings known to potential users outside the museum. Holdings should be announced in appropriate journals and newsletters, and, when appropriate, in the *National Union Catalog of Manuscript Collections*. A brochure describing the archives and its holdings is also recommended, as is a guide to the archives' holdings. The guide, if displayed in appropriate libraries, allows potential users to acquaint themselves with the holdings without visiting the archives, and serves as a great tool for publicizing the program.

The archivist should consider going out into the community to meet with local groups to talk about the history of the museum or the archives program. A symposia series or a lecture series is also worthy of consideration. The archivist should use any appropriate means to reach out to all potential users and supporters on behalf of the archives.

Exhibits are a good way to bring museum archives to the public. *The University Museum, University of Pennsylvania, Philadelphia.*

Bibliography

Archival Forms Manual. Chicago: Society of American Archivists, 1982.

Baum, Willa K. *Oral History for the Local Historical Society.* Nashville: American Association for State and Local History, 1974.

————. *Transcribing and Editing Oral History.* Nashville: American Association for State and Local History, 1977.

Brichford, Maynard. *Archives & Manuscripts: Appraisal & Accessioning.* Chicago: Society of American Archivists, 1977.

Casterline, Gail Farr. *Archives & Manuscripts: Exhibits.* Chicago: Society of American Archivists, 1980.

Clark, Robert L., Jr. (ed.). *Archives-Library Relations.* New York and London: R. R. Bowker Company, 1976.

Collins, Terry, and Steven P. Johnson. *Guide to the Archives of the New York Zoological Society.* New York: New York Zoological Society, 1982.

Draft Guidelines for Botanical Gardens and Arboretum Archives and for Plant Science Society Archives. New York: The New York Botanical Garden Library, 1980.

Duckett, Kenneth W. *Modern Manuscripts: A Practical Manual for Their Management, Care and Use.* Nashville: American Association for State and Local History, 1975.

Evans, Frank B. *Modern Archives and Manuscripts: A Select Bibliography.* Chicago: Society of American Archivists, 1975.

Gracy, David B. *Archives & Manuscripts: Arrangement & Description.* Chicago: Society of American Archivists, 1977.

————. "Starting an Archives." *Georgia Archive* 1 (1972): 20-29.

Guide to the Smithsonian Archives, 1983. Washington: Smithsonian Institution Press, 1983.

Holbert, Sue E. *Archives & Manuscripts: Reference & Access.* Chicago: Society of American Archivists, 1977.

Hoober, David H. "Are You Guilty by Default? An Archivist States the Case for Establishing Institutional Archives." *History News* (May 1983): 17-21.

Johnson, Steven P., and Terry Collins. *Guide to the Archives and Manuscripts of the New York Botanical Garden.* New York: The New York Botanical Garden Library, 1983.

Lytle, Richard H. (ed.). *Management of Archives and Manuscript Collections for Librarians.* Chicago: Society of American Archivists, 1980.

Pederson, Ann, and Gail Farr Casterline. *Archives & Manuscripts: Public Programs.* Chicago: Society of American Archivists, 1982.

Phillips, Venia T., and Maurice E. Phillips. *Guide to the Manuscript Collections of the Academy of Natural Sciences of Philadelphia.* Philadelphia: Academy of Natural Sciences of Philadelphia, 1963.

Registrars' Report. 1:9 (1980). Entire issue devoted to museum archives.

Schellenberg, T. R. *The Management of Archives.* New York: Columbia University Press, 1965.

Schwartz, Carol (ed.). "Keeping Our House in Order: The Importance of Museum Records." *Museum News* 61 (1983): 38-49.

Starting an Archives. Problems in Archives Kits. Chicago: Society of American Archivists, 1980.

Sung, Carolyn Hoover. *Archives & Manuscripts: Reprography.* Chicago: Society of American Archivists, 1982.

Walch, Timothy. *Archives & Manuscripts: Security.* Chicago: Society of American Archivists, 1977.

Appendix A: Archives Policy Statement

MEMORANDUM

DATE:

TO: Members of the professional research staff
          and heads of organization units

FROM: Director
          No-Name Museum (NNM)

SUBJECT: Archives policy statement

    The Museum Archives Program preserves and makes available to
researchers and administrators the historical record of the activities
of the Museum. This includes records of NNM offices, and papers of
NNM staff reflecting their professional activities. The records may
occur in many forms, including for example, correspondence files of
offices and individuals, photographs, audio recordings, and machine
readable records.

    Preservation of the Museum's archives is the joint responsibility
of archivists, curators, and administrators. Always consult the
Museum Archivist when records are to be discarded. This ensures
conformity with the law and Museum policy, and preservation of the
historical record. The Archivist also provides temporary storage for
nonarchival records which must be retained for legal or fiscal
reasons.

    I hope you will take a few minutes to examine the attached
Archives Policy Statement, since the program's success depends on
staff cooperation.

Archives Policy
of the
No-Name Museum

1. DEFINITIONS.

   a. NNM records: All correspondence and other documentation produced in the course of official business of the No-Name Museum.

   b. NNM archives: Those records selected for permanent preservation, usually after they become inactive. Archives assume many forms, including computer records and audio-visual materials.

   c. Professional papers: Personal research notebooks and other records of research created by Museum staff. (See section 3 for distinction between archives and professional papers.)

   d. Manuscript collections or special collections: Papers collected by curators from outside the Museum. These papers usually document the specimen collections.

2. GENERAL POLICY.

   a. Purpose. The No-Name Museum shall preserve its archives and the professional papers of Museum scientists, curators, and honorary associates for their research value. The Museum Archives is the official repository of the No-Name Museum, charged with care of official archives and with soliciting donations of professional papers from staff and associated scholars.

   b. Appraisal of records. All records created or received in the course of official business are the property of the No-Name Museum. When these records become inactive--no longer regularly used by the office or person who created them--they are appraised for continuing research value. Inactive records are:

      (1) discarded in accordance with the law and Museum policy,

      (2) transferred to the central Museum Archives, or

      (3) maintained for research elsewhere in the Museum.

c. Disposal of records. All Museum staff should be aware
    that Museum policy does not permit unauthorized
    destruction, donation, or other dispersal of Museum
    records. The Archivist of the Museum will ensure that
    all disposition of records is consistent with Museum
    policy, and staff members are urged to work with the
    Archivist in records disposition. The Museum Archives
    will always consult appropriate administrators and
    curators when evaluating records for destruction. Once
    records are received in the Archives, they will be
    discarded only with concurrence of the office or person
    that created them.

d. Records management. In the normal course of its work,
    the NNM Archives is involved in records appraisal and
    disposition; assisting NNM staff in timely disposal of
    unneeded records is complementary to ensuring
    preservation of archives.

    The Archives also assists NNM staff with establishment
    and maintenance of files. General assistance is
    available to improve filing systems. Specific
    assistance is given to establish techniques which
    identify inactive records for appraisal and ultimate
    disposition.

    Staff concern for NNM Archives should include preserving
    the order and integrity of records while they are
    current. Since archives are maintained in their
    original arrangement, staff should maintain current
    records in order and transfer intact those records
    selected for archival preservation. The Archivist must
    be consulted before any records are dismantled or
    dispersed.

e. Cooperation with staff. Selection of records for
    preservation--and securing donations of personal
    papers--is a joint effort of staff and Archivist. The
    Archivist relies on the staff member for information
    about the office and its records, and the staff member
    relies on the Archivist for technical assistance and a
    broad view of what should be preserved.

f. Maintaining the order of records. Staff concern for the
    Museum's archives should include preserving the order
    and integrity of records while they are current. Since
    archives are maintained in their original arrangement,
    staff should maintain current records in order and
    transfer intact those records selected for archival
    preservation. The Archivist must be consulted before
    any records are dismantled.

g. Location of archives. Many archives in the Museum must be maintained in the curatorial units, usually because they document the specimen collections. Such collections are processed on location by the Museum Archives and, in conjunction with curators and administrators, made available to users through the Archives finding aids and indexes. A centralized information system for decentralized archives is a necessity. (See 5b below for information about restricted archives.)

3. PROFESSIONAL PAPERS AND NON-ARCHIVAL MATERIALS.

a. Official records vs. professional papers. While some materials are clearly official records and therefore the property of the Museum and others are clearly professional papers, in many cases the distinction is difficult to make. Professional staff members may combine official records and professional papers. Moreover, when research materials document collections, the unit concerned has an interest in their continued preservation at the Museum. These are difficult cases which must be resolved individually. Hopefully, staff will donate their professional papers to the Museum, thereby avoiding problems of segregating professional papers and official records.

b. Non-archival materials defined. Several kinds of material are excluded from the definition of archives:

(1) files collected for information only, for example, a file of laboratory equipment advertisements

(2) extra copies of documents preserved only for reference convenience

(3) stocks of publications

(4) stocks of mimeographed documents

(5) files of reprints

Bring these materials to the attention of the Archives staff before discarding or transferring them to the Archives.

4. SPECIAL COLLECTIONS.

In addition to the personal papers of Museum scholars, the central Archives collects non-Museum papers closely related to Museum activities. Many other manuscripts-- neither official archives nor papers of Museum related scholars--exist throughout the Museum. Papers of

scholars with no Museum connection have been given to
the Museum or have found their way into the Museum's
care. Curators have collected papers related to their
collections or research interests. These manuscript
collections constitute an important part of the Museum's
research collection and should receive proper care. The
Museum Archives is available to assist with professional
care of these manuscript collections. Where the
collections are closely related in subject
matter to the Museum's archives, they should be included
in the Museum Archives information system. In almost
all cases, these collections are not appropriate for
inclusion physically in the Museum Archives depository.

5.   OTHER RESPONSIBILITIES OF THE MUSEUM ARCHIVES.

In addition to preservation activities, the Museum
Archives has several responsibilities to the Museum
staff and others in the scholarly community.

a.   Access to archival holdings. The Archives maintains a
degree of control over its holdings which will ensure
reasonable reference service to staff and other
scholars. the Archives will process selected records in
depth according to demand and potential research value.
The Archives further informs the scholarly community of
the Museum's archival resources through publication of
guides to the archives, regular reporting to the
National Union Catalog of Manuscript Collections, and
communicating with appropriate scholarly journals.

b.   Restrictions. The Archives provides a maximum of
archival resources to staff and scholars, while
protecting rights of privacy and legitimate proprietary
rights by restrictions on access to records. Unless
restrictions are imposed by the donor or transferring
office, research materials are open to all.

c.   Physical security. The Archives provides physical
security for records and personal papers used by
researchers in its reading room.

6.   PROCEDURES FOR SECURING ARCHIVES' SERVICES.

a.   Requesting disposition of papers. Staff who desire to
transfer records or professional papers to the Museum
Archives should submit a written request. An Archivist
will examine the materials with the person in charge.
Both the Archives and the requesting office will benefit
if consultation precedes work on the records.   Records

must not be sent to the Archives unannounced, because the Archives staff needs to examine records with administrators' and curators' assistance before preparation for transfer is made.

b. Determining disposition of papers. Archives staff and curators or administrators will decide on one of several actions:

   (1) Determine that the records are not archival and make legal disposition or transfer to a holding area until legal disposition is possible.

   (2) Determine that the records are archival and transfer them to the Museum Archives.

   (3) Determine that the records are archival and preserve them on location.

   (4) Determine that the records are active and establish a measure to identify inactive records.

c. Donating personal papers. The Archives staff is available to assist in making arrangements for donation of personal papers. Although papers usually do not come to the Archives during the donor's active professional life, early arrangements for giving papers to the Museum at a later date are encouraged. Often the papers will remain in the unit concerned for a period of time after retirement or death of the donor, for use with collections.

Appendix B: Inventory Work Sheet

Date_____   Number_____

RECORD SERIES	ADMINISTRATIVE UNIT
DATES	RESTRICTIONS/SI TITLE
VOLUME	SOURCE OF MATERIAL
ASSOCIATED OBJECTS	OFFICE LOCATION (BUILDING, ROOM NUMBER)
NUMBER AND SIZE OF FILES, DRAWERS OR DOCUMENTS	

DESCRIPTION (TITLE, TYPES OF MATERIAL, NATURE AND DATES OF THE RESPONSIBILITIES OF CREATING OFFICE OR OFFICER, SUBJECTS COVERED, DUPLICATION, MISSING OR PURGED MATERIAL)

ARRANGEMENT

INDEX, FINDING AIDS OR FILE GUIDES

ST-8382
8-15-74

Appendix C: Accession Report

NO-NAME MUSEUM ARCHIVES

ACCESSION REPORT

Accession No.

Donor or Transferring Office and Contact

Type of Transfer (check one)   Transfer Documents

___ SI records·   Records schedule number _____
___ Non-SI records   Date of deed of gift   _____
___ Personal papers   Date of acknowledgment   _____
___ Security deposit

Restrictions

Tentative Title

Approximate Inclusive Dates

Arrangement/Series List

Descriptive Entry

Finding Aids (check all that apply)   Temporary Index Terms

___ Box list
___ Folder list
___ Card index
___ Other (describe)